...FENSHIRE
...ARY &
...ON SERVICES

...DRAWN
...IBRARY

D0358951

THE STORY OF
HIP-HOP

POP HISTORIES

MATT ANNISS

W
FRANKLIN WATTS
LONDON • SYDNEY

First published in 2013 by Franklin Watts

Copyright © 2013 Arcturus Publishing Limited

Franklin Watts
338 Euston Road
London NW1 3BH

Franklin Watts Australia
Level 17/207 Kent Street, Sydney NSW 2000

Produced by Arcturus Publishing Limited,
26/27 Bickels Yard, 151–153 Bermondsey Street, London SE1 3HA

The right of Matt Anniss to be identified as the author of this work has been asserted by him in accordance with the Copyright, Designs and Patents Act 1988.

All rights reserved.

Text: Matt Anniss
Editors: Joe Harris and Rachel Blount
Design: Paul Myerscough and Keith Williams

Picture credits:
Matt Anniss: 7c; Corbis: Gary Gershoff/Retna Ltd. 9, Chi Modu/Diverse Images 4t, Tim Mosenfelder 18b, Michael Ochs Archives 12; Dreamstime: Andres Rodriguez 5b; Fanouninho: 11t; Heavy Rotation: 6; Krijn van Noordwijk 15; Shutterstock: Admedia 13bl, ARS 8b, Arvzdix 24, Andrey Bayda 16t, Christian Bertrand 19, 27b, BMCL 27t, Katrina Brown 18t, S Bukley 11b, 17t, 25b, Michal Durinik 13t, Featureflash 17b, Mat Hayward 28, Kzenon 14b, Loskutnikov 22t, Randy Miramontez 31, Sean Nel 25t, Mr Pics 26, Lev Radin 10, 16b, Adam J. Sablich 1, 23b, Derrick Salters 22b, Joe Seer 7b, 20, Nikola Spasenoski 23t; Wallpapers.free-review.net: 21t; Wikimedia: 8t, Kristof Acke 29t, Jason Anfinsen 21b, Bigtimepeace 4c, Evhead 29b, Javier Mediavilla Ezquibela 13bc, Mikamote 14t, Mika-Photography 5t.
Cover images: Shutterstock: arvzdix top left, Mat Hayward top centre right, Kzenon top centre left, Aija Lehtonen main, Randy Miramontez top far left, Anton Oparin top right, Adam J. Sablich top far right.

A CIP catalogue record for this book is available from the British Library.

Dewey Decimal Classification Number: 781.6'49

ISBN 978 1 4451 1866 6

Printed in China

Franklin Watts is a division of Hachette Children's Books, an Hachette UK company.
www.hachette.co.uk

SL002670EN

Supplier 03, Date 0513, Print Run 2374

ABERDEENSHIRE
LIBRARIES

3109246

Bertrams	24/06/2013
J781.649	£12.99

CONTENTS

BLOCK PARTY ROOTS

Hip-hop is now one of the best-loved musical styles on the planet, and a multi-million dollar industry. Yet it wasn't always this way. In musical terms, hip-hop is a relatively recent development.

Bronx party

The roots of hip-hop lie in the Bronx, a poor area of New York City. There, in the 1970s, a performer called DJ Kool Herc started throwing illegal street parties, known as 'block parties'.

Kool like Hercules

At these block parties, DJ Kool Herc would play popular soul, disco, funk and rock songs of the time. The parties were popular with local teenagers, who would gather to have dancing contests, known as 'battles'.

The origins of mixing

DJ Kool Herc noticed that dancers would respond more favourably to the sections of songs featuring heavy beats. He went away and developed a way of quickly 'mixing' between the breakbeats on popular records by artists such as James Brown a

DJ KOOL HERC THREW THE FIRST EVER HIP-HOP BLOCK PARTIES OUTSIDE THIS BUILDING ON SEDGWICK AVENUE IN THE BRONX, NEW YORK.

POPULAR STYLE

Other DJs soon started copying Kool Herc's style. At block parties across New York, DJs would put on seamless performances, extending popular drumbeats using two vinyl turntables and a basic DJ mixer.

On the microphone

To add something extra to his performances, DJ Kool Herc began reciting short verses of poetry over the beats. This was inspired by music sound system 'deejays' in Jamaica, who would speak or sing over the records they played.

HIP-HOP

...ool Herc i...

...op. H...

...ure

DJ Pre...

Performance poet

Another big influence on DJ Kool Herc was Gil Scott-Heron, a soul artist who spoke rather than sang over music. Gil Scott-Heron thought of himself as a performance poet, rather than a musician. He was arguably the first ever rapper.

Rap attack

This style of speaking over music became known as rapping. Soon, local teenagers began to write their own short verses and ask to rap over Kool Herc's beats at block parties. Hip-hop as we know it today was born.

MANY TEENAGERS AT EARLY HIP-HOP BLOCK PARTIES SHOWED OFF BY PULLING THEIR OWN UNIQUE DANCE MOVES, CALLED 'BREAKDANCING'.

RAPPER'S DELIGHT

By 1978, the new musical style dominating New York's black neighbourhoods had a name: hip-hop. An influential young rapper named Cowboy first used the term at a block party in the Bronx, and it caught on.

SYLVIA'S BIG IDEA

The first hip-hop record ever made wasn't the product of New York's hip-hop DJs and MCs, but rather a businesswoman called Sylvia Robinson. She heard hip-hop DJs and rappers at a party and decided the time was right to record a rap record.

Breakthrough needed

Despite its popularity in New York, hip-hop was almost unknown elsewhere around the world. What the sound needed to go global was a smash hit. That came in 1979.

False start

Sylvia Robinson tried to persuade a well-known local rapper called Fab Five Freddy to record a song, but he wasn't interested. Eventually, she found a trio of young rappers from New Jersey who were willing to perform on her record.

THE SUGARHILL GANG WERE THE FIRST EVER RECORDED HIP-HOP GROUP AND THEY ARE STILL PERFORMING TODAY.

Good times

Robinson's idea was simple: the three rappers would take it in turn to rhyme over a backing track based on Chic's *Good Times*, a popular disco hit. The record was made in an afternoon in Robinson's recording studio.

Massive smash

Within weeks of being released, *Rapper's Delight* by the Sugarhill Gang began to move up the pop charts. It was a hit all over the world and introduced rap to a whole new audience.

A VINYL SUGARHILL GANG RECORD.

Birth of an industry

Rapper's Delight showed young rappers that they could make a living from recording hip-hop songs. Arguably the most significant of these was a group called the Sequence, the world's first all-female rap crew.

● PLAYLIST
OLD SKOOL HIP-HOP

Sugarhill Gang – *Rapper's Delight*
(Sugarhill Records, 1979)

Spoonie Gee – *Spoonin Rap*
(The Sound of New York, 1979)

Lady B – *To the Beat Y'All* (TEC Records, 1979)

Funky Four Plus One – *That's the Joint*
(Sugarhill Records, 1979)

Kurtis Blow – *The Breaks* (Mercury, 1980)

Afrika Bambaata & the Soulsonic Force – *Planet Rock* (Tommy Boy, 1982)

THE INTERNATIONAL SUCCESS OF ARTISTS SUCH AS JAY-Z WOULDN'T HAVE BEEN POSSIBLE WITHOUT THE SUGARHILL GANG.

Trailblazers

Today's hip-hop stars owe a lot to Sylvia Robinson and Sugarhill Records. Without her eye for a business opportunity, hip-hop may never have escaped its New York block party roots.

SCRATCHIN' THAT ITCH

The success of the Sugarhill Gang introduced the world to rap music and hip-hop, and in the years that followed the scene slowly began to grow. However, it was not rappers pushing the sound forward, but rather the DJs.

DJ battle

In an attempt to get one up on Kool Herc, DJs invented new tricks and ways of mixing records together. Grand Wizard Theodore perfected a technique he called 'scratching'. He did this by pushing a vinyl record backwards and forwards to create a unique sound, called a 'scratch'.

THE TECHNIQUE OF SCRATCHING IS STILL USED TODAY IN MANY NIGHTCLUBS AND MUSIC VENUES.

THE ROLAND TR-808 WAS MUCH CHEAPER THAN PREVIOUS DRUM MACHINES, MEANING THAT IT WAS QUICKLY ADOPTED AS A BEAT-MAKING TOOL BY YOUNG HIP-HOP PRODUCERS.

FLASH IS FAST

Grandmaster Flash combined scratching with a new method of mixing called 'cutting'. Cutting is a technique where a snatch of someone rapping or singing or part of the record-scratching sound can be dropped in over a beat.

The first star DJ

Flash's amazing mixing made him the most celebrated hip-hop DJ in New York. The pop band Blondie even mentioned him in one of their songs, *Rapture*. It wasn't long before Sugarhill Records offered Flash a recording contract.

Flash created a revolutionary record called *Grandmaster Flash on the Wheels of Steel*. It was a seven-minute recording of him showing off his DJ skills, cutting, mixing and scratching sections of other people's songs to make a brand new track.

The start of sampling

Grandmaster Flash on the Wheels of Steel was a landmark moment in the history of hip-hop. It proved that DJs could make records and introduced the idea of 'sampling'. This means making new tracks using parts of other songs.

Revolutionary concept

In the years to come, sampling would become the basis of many hip-hop records. Today, many successful rap, pop and R&B tracks are based around samples of familiar records. Flash's big idea changed music forever.

GRANDMASTER FLASH (CENTRE) JOINED FORCES WITH FIVE RAPPERS IN 1978 TO FORM GRANDMASTER FLASH AND THE FURIOUS FIVE.

INSIDE THE SOUND

TURNTABLISM

Turntablism is a kind of performance where DJs show off their skills using two vinyl turntables and a mixer. They use a number of difficult techniques to impress a crowd, including scratching, cutting and 'beat juggling'. Beat juggling is the process of quickly cutting between vinyl records on two different turntables to make a new beat pattern.

WALK THIS WAY

In the early 1980s, hip-hop was growing in popularity but was still largely unknown to most music fans. If it was going to cross over into the mainstream, it needed big stars to take it there.

New arrivals

In 1985, hip-hop's first superstars arrived in the shape of a trio from Queens, New York, called Run DMC. The two rappers and one DJ that made up Run DMC looked like stars. They dressed in sharp Adidas tracksuits and trainers and wore heavy gold chains.

ROCKING OUT

Run DMC also sounded the part. Their songs were catchy but heavy, including sounds more often associated with rock music, such as electric guitars. Because of this, they won many new fans outside of the hip-hop scene. Sales of their *King of Rock* album soared.

Superstars

Music television station MTV had traditionally steered clear of hip-hop, but soon started showing Run DMC videos. Run DMC also became the first hip-hop act to appear on the cover of America's leading music magazine, *Rolling Stone*. Suddenly, hip-hop was big news everywhere.

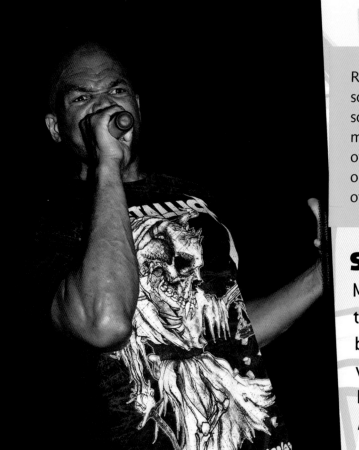

DARREN 'DMC' MCDANIELS OF RUN DMC IS STILL ONE OF THE MOST WIDELY RESPECTED RAPPERS ON THE HIP-HOP SCENE.

My Adidas

Run DMC's success didn't end there. In 1986 they hit the top five in the American charts with *Walk this Way*, a single they recorded with heavy rock group Aerosmith. On the back of this, they secured a $1 million (£600,000) sponsorship deal with Adidas.

THE RUNAWAY SUCCESS OF THE BEASTIE BOYS SHOWED THAT HIP-HOP WAS A STYLE OF MUSIC THAT COULD BE MADE BY ANYONE, WHETHER BLACK OR WHITE.

The new style

Just as Run DMC hit the heights, another group burst into the limelight: the Beastie Boys. Like Run DMC, the Beastie Boys crossed hip-hop with rock music. But the Beastie Boys were different— they were white.

Everything changes

The Beastie Boys *Licensed to Ill* became the biggest-selling hip-hop album of the 1980s. It inspired a whole generation of white teenagers to listen to hip-hop and turned rock fans into rap fans. Hip-hop was now firmly established as one of the most popular forms of music in the world.

HIP-HOP HEROES

KID ROCK ON THE BEASTIE BOYS

'The first time I ever saw the Beastie Boys on stage my jaw dropped to the floor! I said to myself "there are white kids that rap – wow!" My mind was blown.'

Kid Rock (pictured)

FIGHT THE POWER

Just as the Beastie Boys and Run DMC were taking rap music to new heights of commercial success, a very different kind of hip-hop group were getting ready to step out of the shadows.

Different perspective

Public Enemy didn't have any time for the kind of rap music offered by the Beastie Boys and Run DMC. They believed that hip-hop songs shouldn't be about having fun. Instead, they wanted to reflect the reality of life for black Americans.

Reflecting life

Public Enemy's front man, Chuck D, believed that rap songs should be used to reflect personal experiences. For many black Americans, that meant poverty, crime, drugs and daily struggles with the authorities.

Hard hitting

The group released their first album, *Yo! Bumrush the Show*, in 1987. It contained hard-hitting raps from Chuck D, Professor Griff and Flavor Flav, and heavy music based around many different samples of other people's music.

THANKS TO THEIR WORK RAISING AWARENESS OF ISSUES THAT AFFECT BLACK AMERICANS, PUBLIC ENEMY ARE NOW CONSIDERED TO BE HIP-HOP LEGENDS.

Sample magic

Sampling was already an established way of making hip-hop tracks. However, Public Enemy's producers, the Bomb Squad, took this to extremes. Some of their tracks featured over 20 or 30 different samples.

IN 2012, PUBLIC ENEMY HEADED OUT ON A WORLD TOUR TO CELEBRATE 25 YEARS OF PUSHING HIP-HOP'S BOUNDARIES.

Rebel without a pause

Yo! Bumrush the Show was a landmark album, but it didn't sell that well. For the follow-up album, *It Takes a Nation of Millions to Hold Us Back*, Chuck D decided to push the limits of hip-hop even further. That meant tackling even more controversial subjects.

PUBLIC ENEMY FRONT MAN CHUCK D NOW SPENDS AS MUCH TIME TALKING TO POLITICIANS ABOUT BLACK AMERICAN ISSUES AS HE DOES PERFORMING.

Public Enemy number one

On the back of *It Takes a Nation of Millions*, Public Enemy became big stars. They proved that rap music could be used as a form of protest and tackle difficult subjects. Hip-hop would never be the same again.

LIVING LEGEND

CHUCK D

Chuck D is one of the most outspoken and controversial rappers of all time. Since finding fame with Public Enemy in the 1980s, he has continued to rap about serious topics affecting the lives of black Americans. This has made him an inspiration to many young rappers. He continues to perform today, and in 2012 released the 12th Public Enemy album, *Most of My Heroes Still Don't Appear on No Stamp*.

HARDCORE HIP-HOUSE

Thanks to Public Enemy and Run DMC, in the late 1980s hip-hop was more respected and successful than ever before. It also rediscovered its dance music roots with a brand new style: hip-house.

Back to the party

Although Public Enemy and others were taking hip-hop away from its dance floor roots, it remained popular in nightclubs. Often, DJs would play hip-hop records alongside other popular dance music sounds. At the tail end of the 1980s, these dance sounds were house music.

THE JUNGLE BROTHERS SCORED A MASSIVE POP HIT IN 1989 WITH *I'LL HOUSE YOU*, PROBABLY THE MOST FAMOUS HIP-HOUSE RECORD OF ALL TIME.

DURING THE HIP-HOUSE YEARS, RAPPERS PERFORMING IN NIGHTCLUBS BECAME A REGULAR SIGHT.

Let there be house

House was massively popular in the 1980s. It had been invented in Chicago around 1985, and by 1987 had begun to dominate the pop charts in Europe. It had little in common with hip-hop and used different types of beats and sounds.

Get busy

As the first New York rappers had performed over disco, funk and soul records, dominant forms of dance music at the time, it was only a matter of time before someone tried to fuse house with hip-hop.

Rockin' the house

Surprisingly, the first 'house rap' record wasn't made by Americans, but by a British group called Beatmasters. They asked two female rappers called the Cookie Crew to rap over a house tune they'd made. *Rok Da House* was a big hit and inspired the new style, hip-house.

INSIDE THE SOUND

HIP-HOUSE

Most traditional hip-hop music is based around beats that borrow the loose rhythms of soul and funk, slowed down to make them easier to rap over. Hip-house is usually faster, and based around the simpler beats of house. This makes the sounds more appealing to dancers.

LET IT ROLL

In the years that followed, hip-house became popular around the world. Rappers such as Tyree Cooper, Queen Latifah, Doug Lazy and Salt 'N' Peppa became household names because of big hip-house club hits.

Return of the rap

In recent years, the idea of fusing rap with dance music has once again become popular. Snoop Dogg, P Diddy and Dizzee Rascal have all made records with top dance music producers, while The Black Eyed Peas make songs that fuse pop, dance and rap.

ALTHOUGH NOW A WORLD-FAMOUS HOUSE DJ, TODD TERRY STARTED LIFE MAKING HIP-HOP BEATS AND EARLY HIP-HOUSE RECORDS.

EAST COAST VS WEST COAST

T he late 1980s saw the birth of an aggressive and controversial new style of music called 'gangsta rap'. Over the next 10 years it would go on to become the dominant force in hip-hop.

DURING THE GANGSTER RAP YEARS, NEW YORK'S RAPPERS FACED STIFF COMPETITION FROM THOSE IN LOS ANGELES, ON AMERICA'S WEST COAST.

Hardcore hip-hop

The roots of gangsta rap lie in the New York hip-hop scene of the mid 1980s, where Boogie Down Productions and Schoolly D created a gritty new style called 'hardcore hip-hop'. They wrote songs that talked about guns, violence and murder.

Far out

On the opposite coast of the United States, in Compton, Los Angeles, a group called NWA were inspired by the New York sound. They set out to push the limits of hardcore hip-hop.

Original gangsters

They achieved just that with their first album, *Straight Outta Compton*. A gory celebration of gang culture in Los Angeles, it sold in huge numbers and introduced the world to West Coast gangsta rap.

ICE-T WAS ONE OF LOS ANGELES' ORIGINAL GANGSTER RAPPERS AND HELPED POPULARISE THE STYLE.

Stars of Death Row

In the years that followed, gangsta rap became the dominant form of hip-hop. Los Angeles' Death Row Records led the charge, turning West Coast rappers Snoop Dogg, Tupac '2Pac' Shakur and Ice-T into global superstars.

HIP-HOP HEROES

SNOOP DOG ON 2PAC

'I truly believe there will never be another rapper who can uplift spirits and explain the ups and downs of everyday life like him.'

Snoop Dogg (pictured)

CONTROVERSY

From the start, gangsta rap was hugely controversial. Due to the violent subject matter, radio and television stations refused to play the songs or videos. However, this didn't stop the CDs selling in huge numbers.

Violent endings

Many people think that the feud between the two record labels may have led to the murders of gangsta rap's two biggest stars. Tupac Shakur was shot dead in Las Vegas in 1996. A year later, Biggie Smalls was murdered in similar circumstances.

THE RISE OF MODERN DAY GANGSTER RAPPERS SUCH AS 50 CENT PROVES THAT THE STYLE IS STILL HUGELY POPULAR.

Bitter rivalry

In the early 1990s, New York's hardcore hip-hop scene began to hit back. The city's Bad Boy Records, home to gangsta rap heavyweight Biggie Smalls (also known as the Notorious B.I.G.), emerged as a major rival to Death Row Records. Soon, a bitter feud developed between the two companies.

FLOWER POWER

The late 1980s and the early 1990s were a golden era for hip-hop. While gangsta rap dominated the sales charts, many new movements emerged that then pulled hip-hop in new directions.

Going underground

One of the biggest underground hip-hop movements of the time was what some called 'conscious' hip-hop. Pioneered by New York acts De La Soul and A Tribe Called Quest, it was almost the polar opposite of gangsta rap.

ALONG WITH DE LA SOUL, A TRIBE CALLED QUEST USHERED IN A NEW GOLDEN ERA OF CONSCIOUS HIP-HOP IN THE LATE 1980S AND EARLY 1990S.

Love and peace

While gangsta rappers were aggressive and talked about violence, the lyrics of De La Soul and A Tribe Called Quest songs were often more inventive. Songs by conscious hip-hop groups were much more positive than gangsta rap records.

THE INVENTION OF THE PORTABLE BOOMBOX MEANT THAT PEOPLE COULD LISTEN TO THEIR FAVOURITE HIP-HOP MUSIC ON THE STREETS.

HIPPY BEAT

The record that heralded the arrival of this new style of hip-hop was De La Soul's 1989 album *Three Feet High and Rising*. Influenced by the hippie 'flower power' movement of the 1960s, it mixed warm, laid back music with quirky and occasionally funny raps about love and life.

NEARLY 25 YEARS AFTER RECORDING THEIR FIRST TRACKS, DE LA SOUL CONTINUE TO PERFORM AT MUSIC FESTIVALS AROUND THE WORLD.

Greater consciousness

A Tribe Called Quest grew up with De La Soul and made similarly laid-back music. They released their first album, *People's Instinctive Travels and the Paths of Rhythm*, in 1990. It once again proved that great rap music didn't have to be about guns and gangs.

PLAYLIST
1990s HIP-HOP

A Tribe Called Quest – *Can I Kick It?*
(Jive, 1990)

Jazzy Jeff and the Fresh Prince – *Summertime* (Jive, 1991)

De La Soul – *Ring Ring Ring (Ha Ha Hey)* (Tommy Boy, 1991)

Craig Mack – *Flava in Your Ear* (Bad Boy Records, 1994)

Nas – *If I Ruled the World* (Columbia Records, 1996)

The Fresh Prince

Another act keen to put fun back into hip-hop was Jazzy Jeff and the Fresh Prince. After recording a number of chart hits they were offered the chance to star in their own television comedy. *The Fresh Prince of Bel Air* was the world's first hip-hop sitcom.

MTV raps

The popularity of hip-hop was helped by increased television exposure. MTV now had its own weekly hip-hop show, *Yo! MTV Raps*. For the first time, millions of TV viewers had access to the latest rap songs.

DON'T FORGET ABOUT DRE

During the 1990s and early 2000s, one man more than any other dominated the hip-hop scene. A former gangsta rapper turned music producer and businessman, Dr Dre launched the careers of many of today's most successful rap stars.

Electro roots

Born Andre Young, Dr Dre first tasted success as part of the 1980s electro group World Class Wreckin' Cru. However, it was with the influential gangsta rap group NWA that he really made his name.

As one of hip-hop's original star makers, Dr Dre is still one of the most influential figures in the rap scene.

Star producer

Not only was Dre one of NWA's rappers, he also produced their music: he took charge of the recording of their songs, and shaped the way that they sounded. When their albums performed well, many other rappers started asking Dre to produce their records.

THE BIRTH OF G-FUNK

Dre developed his own particular take on hip-hop. Called 'G-Funk', it was slow, bass-heavy and featured samples from 1970s and 1980s electro-funk music. He first showcased the sound on his 1993 album *The Chronic*, which helped launch the careers of rappers Snoop Dogg and Nate Dogg.

EMINEM on DR DRE

'It was an honour to hear the words out of Dre's mouth that he liked my music. Growing up, I wanted to be Dr Dre. He's the biggest hip-hop producer ever.'

Eminem (pictured)

Star maker

The release of Dre's album *The Chronic* made all of its rappers into big stars. Dre decided to launch his own record label, Aftermath, where he could combine making records with producing songs for other people.

The real Slim Shady

One of these people was an unknown rapper from Detroit called Eminem. Dre produced his first single, *My Name Is*, and most of *The Slim Shady LP*, his first album, in 1999. Within a year, Eminem was one of the biggest hip-hop stars on the planet.

Powerful producer

Following the success of Eminem's first album, Dre decided to concentrate on production. In the years that followed, he launched the career of 50 Cent and worked with big stars such as Jay-Z, Timbaland and Raekwon. Today, he's still one of the most in-demand producers in the rap music industry.

THANKS TO THE SUPPORT OF DR DRE, EMINEM HAS BECOME ONE OF THE MOST POPULAR RAPPERS IN THE WORLD.

BIG BUSINESS

As the 1990s turned to the 2000s, rap records were dominating the charts. As a result, rappers from the streets of New York or Los Angeles could become millionaires. The era of 'bling' had begun.

Making money

Rappers who had once talked about life in poor areas were now rapping about money, cars and women. Many people in the underground hip-hop scene saw this as selling out. The rappers who were topping the charts didn't care; after all, they were living the high life!

Rap businessmen

Many of the most successful rappers of the period were also businessmen. Many had invested their earnings in starting companies. Sean Combs, sometimes known as P Diddy, built a fortune on the success of his label Bad Boy Records.

SEAN 'P DIDDY' COMBS HAS MADE MILLIONS OF DOLLARS FROM HIS SEAN JOHN CLOTHING AND FRAGRANCE RANGE.

ROC AND ROLL

Another rapper who proved to be a smart businessman was Jay-Z. He decided to take on Sean Combs and Dr Dre by starting a record label called Roc-A-Fella. It was a roaring success and launched the careers of Kanye West, Foxy Brown and Freeway.

Business success

Running a record label was never going to be enough for this new crop of hip-hop businessmen. Slowly and surely, they began to use their fame and popularity to start many other types of companies.

Fashion leader

Sean Combs was one of the first rap stars to start his own clothing label, Sean John, in 1998. It was a roaring success from the start, and has helped him to amass a fortune of well over $500 million (£310 million).

AS ONE OF THE MOST SUCCESSFUL FEMALE RAPPERS OF ALL TIME, MISSY ELLIOT IS PAID MILLIONS OF DOLLARS TO ADVERTISE ADIDAS SPORTSWEAR.

Hip-hop businesswoman

Missy Elliot, the most successful female rapper of all time, has also cashed in on her fame. Since the early 2000s, she has designed a number of clothing ranges for Adidas.

LIVING LEGEND

JAY-Z Shawn 'Jay-Z' Carter got his break in hip-hop performing on stage with rap legend Big Daddy Kane in the early 1990s. When he couldn't find a record deal, he started his own label, Roc-A-Fella, in 1995. He became a global rap star and used his earnings to launch a fashion business, Rocawear. In 2008, he married R&B star Beyoncé.

TALK ABOUT POP MUSIC

Since the turn of the century, hip-hop has continued to evolve. Now, the boundary lines between rap, pop and dance are more blurred than ever. In the twenty-first century, hip-hop and pop are almost the same thing.

Be my guest

The late 1990s and early 2000s saw a rise in rappers making guest appearances on R&B, soul and pop records. Jay-Z and P Diddy led the way, appearing on songs by the likes of Beyoncé, R Kelly, Mariah Carey and Michael Jackson.

TO THE FRONT

Jay-Z also appeared on *Frontin*, a 2003 hit single for Pharrell Williams, one of the men behind production group The Neptunes. The group would go on to be key figures in the fusion of hip-hop and pop music.

BEYONCÉ HAS WORKED WITH MANY DIFFERENT RAPPERS ON HER TRACKS, INCLUDING HER HUSBAND JAY-Z.

Neptunes' palace

Producers The Neptunes grew up listening to hip-hop, pop, soul, funk and rock music. Their unique musical style blended all of these elements. Soon, they became the most in-demand producers in the world, making music for the likes of Kelis, Usher and Destiny's Child.

West is best

The man who did most to redefine hip-hop as pop music was Kanye West. In the early 2000s he experimented with using pop elements in his tracks. In 2008, this led to the release of *808s and Heartbreak*, a straightforward pop album.

Big influence

808s and Heartbreak was not hugely popular and sold poorly compared to Kanye West's other albums. However, it proved to rap acts that they could make pop songs if they wanted to.

FEW RAP ACTS HAVE BEEN QUITE AS SUCCESSFUL AT FUSING RAP WITH POP AND DANCE ACTS AS THE BLACK EYED PEAS.

Black Eyed beats

One band that took up the challenge laid down by Kanye West was The Black Eyed Peas. After Kanye West's change of heart, they followed suit, filling their 2009 album *The END* with catchy dance songs. Since then they have dominated the pop charts worldwide.

LIVING LEGEND

KANYE WEST

Kanye West first rose to prominence not as a rapper, but a music producer. In the 1990s, he was responsible for many of the biggest hits on Jay-Z's Roc-A-Fella label. In 2004, he released his debut album, *The College Drop Out*. Since then, he has sold more than 30 million albums.

PUSHING BOUNDARIES

While Jay-Z, Kanye West and The Black Eyed Peas were tearing up the pop charts, a whole new generation of underground rappers and producers were reinventing hip-hop. As a result, many fresh new styles of rap music have emerged.

INSIDE THE SOUND

GRIME

Grime differs from hip-hop in the sound of the beats and music over which rappers perform. Instead of hip-hop beats, the grooves used by grime rappers are influenced by dance music styles such as drum and bass and garage. Most grime tracks feature dark electronic sounds.

Wonky beats

In Los Angeles and New York, a sound has developed called 'wonky' or 'glitch-hop'. This blends experimental electronic sounds with hip-hop beats. The wonky sound is far removed from the polished pop of today's global rap superstars.

AFTER EMERGING FROM THE UNDERGROUND GRIME SCENE, WILEY AND TINCHEY STRIDER HAVE BECOME POP STARS IN THE UK.

GRITTY RAPS ABOUT LIFE IN THE EAST END OF LONDON MIXED WITH GARAGE AND ELECTRO BEATS WERE THE START OF THE GRIME MUSIC SCENE.

To the dancefloor

The grime scene's two most popular rappers, Wiley and Dizzee Rascal, quickly became household names in the UK. After finding fame, both decided to create dance records, making grime-style hip-house records with well-known dance music producers.

Electronic experiments

Wonky and glitch-hop producers such as Flying Lotus and Prefuse 73 are influenced by electronica and indie rock artists such as Aphex Twin and Radiohead. In turn, they have influenced a whole new generation of producers from around the world, such as Hudson Mohawke and Rustie from Scotland.

Going *Bonkers*

Dizzee Rascal's *Bonkers*, a record he made with American house producer Armand Van Helden, became a worldwide hit. He even performed it at the opening ceremony of the 2012 Olympics, which took place in East London, close to where grime was first developed 10 years earlier.

It's a London thing

In London, England, far away from hip-hop's American base, young British rappers and producers have been making their own rap records for years. By the early 2000s, hip-hop in the UK had developed its own unique sound – grime.

DIZZEE RASCAL WAS THE FIRST GRIME RAPPER TO ENJOY SUCCESS IN THE POP CHARTS, AND BECAME ONE OF THE UK'S BRIGHTEST HIP-HOP STARS.

EASTERN ELECTRICS

Grime was different to anything that had come before. Developed in Bow in East London, it mixed gritty raps about life with gritty, bass heavy beats influenced by popular dance music styles such as garage and electro. It was like nothing the world had heard before.

HIP-HOP PLANET

What started out on the streets of the Bronx in New York in the 1970s has now become a global musical force. Hip-hop is now as much of a worldwide musical style as rock, pop or dance music.

European rap

Nowadays, many countries have their own hip-hop scenes, with rappers recording songs in their own language. Hip-hop is particularly big in France and Germany, where many of the scene's biggest stars are not global icons but homegrown rappers.

SNOW BUSINESS

Since the early 2000s, many underground hip-hop acts have emerged from Scandinavian countries Sweden and Denmark. Rap is becoming increasingly popular in other European countries, especially in Russia and the Netherlands, where MC Brainpower is a huge star.

African rhythms

A great example of how rap music is being fused with both modern and traditional music from around the world can be found in Portugal. There, a band with African origins called Buraka Som Sistema have forged a sound that blends rap music with Algerian kuduro music and dance beats.

PEOPLE ALL OVER THE WORLD ENJOY DANCING TO THE MANY DIFFERENT SOUNDS OF HIP-HOP AT NIGHTCLUBS.

Global influences

Rappers born in the UK and America are mixing hip-hop with world music sounds. MIA, a UK rapper with Sri Lankan parents, has been successful thanks to a unique style that mixes traditional Asian music with rap and grime-style beats.

Big in Japan

The biggest hip-hop scene outside the USA can be found in Japan. The country is home to some of the best hip-hop DJs around. Many Japanese DJs have won the DMC World Championships, the annual competition to find the world's best scratch DJ.

Worldwide family

Although American rappers and producers still dominate the pop charts around the world, hip-hop music is now made, played and celebrated in almost every country on earth. What DJ Kool Herc started has become a truly global phenomenon.

JAPANESE SCRATCH DJ KID KOALA TRAVELS AROUND THE WORLD, PLAYING TO PACKED AUDIENCES, OFTEN WHILE WEARING A BEAR COSTUME!

RAPPER MIA HAS DEVELOPED A CUTTING-EDGE STYLE OF HIP-HOP THAT BORROWS ELEMENTS FROM GRIME, ELECTRO-HOUSE AND TRADITIONAL SRI LANKAN MUSIC.

● PLAYLIST
GLOBAL HIP-HOP

Brainpower – *Boks Ouwe*
(Netherlands – Lyric Recordings, 2008)

Buraka Som Sistema – *Sound of Kudoro*
(Portugal – Fabric Records, 2007)

DJ Cleo – *FaceBook*
(South Africa – Will of Steel Productions, 2009)

King Giddra – *9-11*
(Japan – Defstar Records, 2002)

La Rumeur – *Inscrivez Greffier*
(France – EMI France, 2004)

GLOSSARY

Commercial success Selling a lot of something, for example CDs and concert tickets.

Controversial Something that divides opinion and stirs up emotions.

DJ Someone who plays music to people for a living. DJ stands for 'disk jockey'.

Electro A style of music popular in the 1980s, based on electronic sounds from drum machines and synthesisers (electronic keyboards).

Electronica A style of music made using computers and electronic instruments.

Evolve To change over time.

Experimental Something that pushes the accepted limits of music or any other art form.

Exposure Widespread discussion of something, for example in newspapers or on television.

Fusion Putting two or more things together, such as styles of music, to make something new.

Illegal Against the law.

Influential Something that inspires people to do similar things, such as to write a song in the same style.

Militant Extreme and forceful.

Mixing The process of blending two songs together during a DJing performance.

Pioneer To do something before anyone else.

Producer A person who specialises in making, or producing, music.

Quirky Odd or eccentric.

R&B A popular form of soul music, often featuring slow beats.

Reciting Reading something out loud.

Revolutionary Something that is so significant that it changes history, or the way people think.

Seamless Smooth or near perfect.

Underground Something that is not well known, and usually popular only with a small group of people.

Vinyl records Pressed black plastic discs used to play music before the invention of CDs. Vinyl records are still popular with DJs and record collectors.

Vinyl turntable A piece of equipment used to play vinyl records.

FURTHER INFORMATION

Books

Hip-Hop America by Nelson George
(Penguin Books, 2005)

Hip-Hop Culture by Wendy Garofoli
(Rainhill, 2011)

The Hip-Hop Scene by Anne Graham
Gaines & Reggie Majors (Enslow, 2009)

History of Hip-Hop – The Roots of Rap by
Thomas Hatch (Red Brick Learning, 2005)

The History of Modern Music by
Matt Anniss (Franklin Watts, 2012)

*The Story of Hip Hop – From Africa
to America, Sugarhill to Eminem* by
Jim Haskins (Puffin Books, 2002)

Websites

www.hip-hop.com
*This leading online rap site features
exclusive video features, news
articles and picture galleries.*

www.hotnewhiphop.com
*A great site that showcases the latest
rap tracks and hip-hop mixtapes
from top stars, unknown DJs and
underground heroes.*

www.rap.about.com
*Discover everything you need to know
about rap and hip-hop, including lists of
the best albums and songs of all time.*

www.rapmusic.com
*An excellent website dedicated to
celebrating the best in rap music,
featuring battle videos and reviews
of the latest hip-hop releases.*

INDEX

SERIES CONTENTS

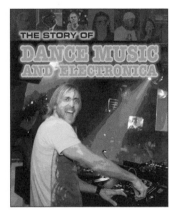

The Story of Dance Music and Electronica

The Dawn of the DJ • The Synthesiser Revolution • Let There be House • Into the Future • This is Acid • Hardcore Uproar • Chill Out • Going Live • Superstar DJs, Here We Go! • Panic at the Disco! • Bass, How Low Can You Go? • Heroes of the Pop Charts • Dance Planet

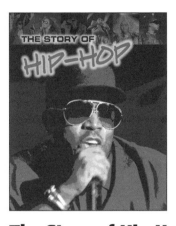

The Story of Hip-Hop

Block Party Roots • Rapper's Delight • Scratchin' that Itch • Walk this Way • Fight the Power • Hardcore Hip-House • East Coast Vs West Coast • Flower Power • Don't Forget about Dre • Big Business • Talk about Pop Music • Pushing Boundaries • Hip-Hop Planet

The Story of Pop Music

The Pre-History of Pop • Rock Around the Clock • On the Box • Girls and Boys • Pop Art • The Age of Glamour • The Synth-Pop Scene • Video Killed the Radio Star • When Will I be Famous? • The Puppet Masters • It's Talent that Matters • Urban All Stars • Talk About Pop Music

The Story of Punk and Indie

Downtown Revolution • Anarchy in the UK • Do It Yourself • Post-Punk • Indie-Pop and Gothic Rock • The Birth of Alternative Rock • Start the Dance • Alternative Goes Mainstream • The Birth of Britpop • Stadium Punk • What Goes Around, Comes Around • When I Ruled the World • Evolving Sounds

The Story of Rock Music

Blues Roots • Rock and Roll Revolution • The British Invasion • Open Your Mind • Living for the Weekend • Glam It Up • Progress • Getting Heavy • Stadium Rock! • Alternative Rock • Changing of the Guard • Looking Back to Look Forward • It's All Rock

The Story of Soul and R&B

The Roots of Soul • The First Soul Stars • The Hit Factory • Funk Brothers and Soul Sisters • Making a Point • The Sound of Philadelphia • You Should be Dancing • Rip It Up and Start Again • Blue-Eyed Soul • Swing Thing • Brand Neo • R&B Goes Global • Big Business